A Year in the Life of Beth Chatto's Gardens

A Year in the Life of
Beth Chatto's Gardens

Photographs by Rachel Warne

Words by Fergus Garrett

Foreword by Beth Chatto

F

FRANCES LINCOLN LIMITED
PUBLISHERS

Contents

Frances Lincoln Limited
4 Torriano Mews
Torriano Avenue
London NW5 2RZ
www.frances-lincoln.com

A Year in the Life of Beth Chatto's Gardens

First Frances Lincoln edition 2012

A catalogue record for this book is available from the British Library.

Designed by Anne Wilson

ISBN 9780 7112 3214 3

Printed and bound in China

1 2 3 4 5 6 7 8 9

PAGE 1 *Bergenia* 'Admiral' and *Deschampsia cespitosa* 'Goldschleier'.
TITLE PAGE *Rhus typhina* in front of an ancient oak tree.
OPPOSITE *Fritillaria verticillata.*

Plan of the Gardens

DRY NURSERY
STOCK BEDS

ENTRANCE

NURSERY

TEA
ROOMS

SCREE
GARDEN

GRAVEL GARDEN

HOUSE

WATER GARDEN

DAMP NURSERY
STOCK BEDS

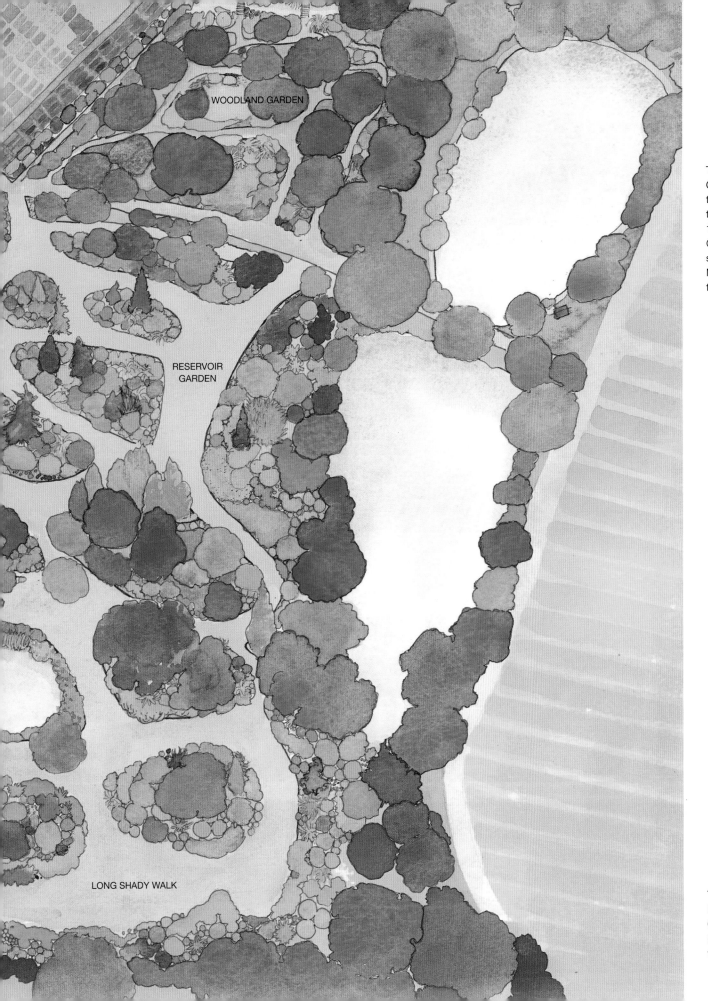

WOODLAND GARDEN

RESERVOIR
GARDEN

LONG SHADY WALK

This plan shows Beth Chatto's gardens as they are today in 2012. Beth began the Woodland Garden in 1989. In 1991 she made the Gravel Garden and in 1998 she converted the former Mediterranean Garden into the Scree Garden.

The Beth Chatto Gardens
Elmstead Market
Colchester
Essex CO7 7DB
www.bethchatto.co.uk

Foreword

I often say a garden is not a picture confined to a frame left hanging on a wall; it is something that changes constantly with the movement of light and the passing of time. To Rachel Warne I am deeply grateful for capturing the many moods and atmospheres experienced during one year, which never will be seen exactly the same again. I am not a photographer so cannot do justice to the skills and techniques involved, but I admire Rachel's work, not only for her choice of subjects but also for her ability to catch something of the spirit of the garden that stirs my emotions. I think this is because she becomes emotionally involved too, as, kneeling at ground level, she explores the fragility of some tiny plant, or, standing pressed against a tree trunk, she feels the rough pattern of ridged bark.

Mine is not an easy garden in which to find conventional, cosy pictures. In place of a framework of hard landscaping I tend to use big, bold plants as focal points, and, of course, with the changing seasons some of these come and go.

I love Rachel's plant portraits, never blown up out of proportion, always taken *in situ*, as, on hands and knees, she spots some delicate piece of embroidery sheltered among more robust neighbours. Her work is honest; sometimes even too honest, maybe? As when I for one might have gone ahead and snipped off some fading stems in an otherwise spring-fresh combination. Some of her pictures make me want to simplify some of the planting, or add something eye-catching, such as a hosta or a dramatic vertical grass, to provide a focal point. It is then that I recall Graham Stuart Thomas's invaluable advice to someone worried about a border that would not come right: he pointed out that it contained no leaf larger than privet:

it needed something to break up the busy effect. Bold foliage, or a completely different shape, such as a strong vertical, will act like a full stop at the end of a fussy sentence. In the Gravel Garden plants such as lavenders, ballota and santolina tend to look like a tray of buns, unless they are interrupted by plants with striking presence, such as ornamental alliums, shimmering grasses or stately verbascums.

This book is more than a record of one year's planting seen throughout the seasons. It is a story, as Rachel, with her artistic eye, discovers new views that I had not noticed before, or captures the change of mood as one walks from the scented heat of the Gravel Garden down a gentle slope into the cool atmosphere of the Water Garden. Here the grass remains green throughout the regular droughts of summer, fed by underground springs lying more than 6 metres/20 feet below the Gravel Garden above. The original ditch, dug to partially drain this low-lying piece of land, was dammed to form four large ponds where moisture-loving plants thrive which never would survive elsewhere in the areas of pure sand and gravel. Sunlight and shadows make patterns across smooth grassy slopes; varied shapes and textures create scenes of gentle tranquillity throughout summer and autumn.

I hope that, as you turn the pages of this book, you will share with me some of the moods and memories that Rachel has recorded.

Beth Chatto
Elmstead Market
Essex
August 2011

Introduction

Beth Chatto is one of life's great givers. To be in her company, listening to her talk, seeing the world through her wise eyes, discussing life, or just being, is a profound experience. And through her work, articles, books, lectures, nursery and gardens, Beth has changed the way the world thinks about gardening. Putting the right plant in the right place and with the right partners has been her passion. But her impact goes deeper. She has made gardeners look at plants in a different way, so broadening our horizons and widening our palette. She is one of the finest, most significant and most influential gardeners of all time.

Born on 27 June 1923, Beth was fortunate to have gardening parents. As a young child she had a small garden of her own; the seed was sown. In 1943 Beth married Andrew Chatto, an Essex fruit farmer. Andrew had been deeply interested in native wild plants and plant communities in their natural habitats ever since as a child on holiday in California he recognized, growing along the roadsides, garden plants such as *Ceanothus* and the orange poppy, *Eschscholzia californica*, which his parents grew in their garden in Radlett, Hertfordshire. His fascinated realization that here they were natives began a life's work. For over fifty years Andrew researched the origins of garden plants, often translating works by French and German travellers and missionaries, and he taught himself Russian in order to be able to read the splendid ecological survey of the USSR. The influence of this research on Beth's gardening life was immense. The environmental requirements of plants, placing them in appropriate conditions to suit their needs by mimicking and mirroring their wild environments, and the interaction of plant communities formed the basic underlying principles of Beth's gardening style.

In the early 1960s the young couple built a split-level house on the wasteland at the far end of Andrew's fruit farm five miles east of Colchester in the village of Elmstead Market. Beth wanted a garden. The site was a wilderness, entirely overgrown with blackthorn, brambles and willows underneath an over-storey of ancient oaks. And it posed many problems. The bleak easterly winds gusting off the Continent, an annual average rainfall

The Gravel Garden at its most colourful, in high summer, with the deep magenta flowers of *Gladiolus communis* subsp. *byzantinus*, white *Allium nigrum* and purple *A. cristophii*, dark blue *Veronica austriaca* 'Kapitän' and *Salvia officinalis* 'Albiflora'.

of only 50 centimetres/20 inches, hungry soils ranging from sand and gravel to silt and clay were bound to prove difficult for many highly bred ornamental plants. But Beth was tireless and of strong constitution. Backed by Andrew, she slowly turned the disadvantages into advantages. The scrub was cleared, the poor ground fed, and the good oaks were left to give structure and form, a comforting canopy. Many of the original oaks, some hundreds of years old, remain today, majestic guardians of the land around them. Several other trees have joined the silhouette, painting the sky (as Beth puts it) and enriching the framework within which the gardens rest. The extreme conditions of the site have been adapted to provide a home for a wide range of plants specifically adapted to and revelling in their habitat.

The gentle slope and contours around the house were harnessed with shallow steps and terraces, made by Andrew and Beth and a cement mixer. Beth then transformed this free-draining, sun-baked area into a Mediterranean-style garden. Against a backdrop that contrasted mounds of cistuses, santolinas and hebes with upright spikes of yuccas, junipers and grasses, she wove a flowing tapestry of jewel-like flowers. With self-sowing poppies, magenta gladioli, alliums, irises, acid-green spurges and pots on the terrace, she was beginning to create her paradise.

Immediately below this area, a stream fed a boggy piece of land, where cows once grazed sunk up to their udders in black mud. The stream was dammed and a series of four clay-lined ponds formed. The interconnected oasis of water became the focus of a lush damp garden. The ponds were punctuated with the sumptuous greenery of aquatic and marginal plants in and adjacent to the water: prehistoric gunneras, towering swamp cypresses, fountains of bamboos.

Although Andrew's influence on Beth and her gardens cannot be overestimated, there were other mentors and influences that contributed significantly to her gardening life. Before marriage Beth attended teacher training college, and teaching has never left her. Education is in her blood and Beth is a born communicator both orally and on paper. Descriptive writing comes easily to her (she may deny this); she is sharply observant, and has an unparalleled gift for summing up in words the intrinsic qualities of a plant. Her books and nursery catalogues are rich with descriptive gems. For example, she writes of *Molinia caerulea* subsp. *arundinacea* 'Transparent': 'Above low, neat clumps of narrow ribbon-shaped leaves stand tall, rigid, knitting-needle-like stems topped with lace-fine heads of tiny rice-like seed cases densely set on hair-thin stems, creating a more gauzy effect. The whole making an exquisite screen when still or when seen bowing and dancing in the wind.' Of *Pennisetum orientale* she says: 'For this grass I welcome a warm, dry summer when hummocks of fine, narrow leaves become crowned with flower heads. They dangle, fat and hairy, like soft grey-mauve caterpillars suspended from thin, wiry stems.' And *Tricyrtis ohsumiensis* she describes as 'An exotic-looking plant for cool, shady conditions and damp leaf-mould soil. Pairs of rich green, pointed leaves facing opposite ways are wrapped round the stem, each forming a cradle for butter-yellow, lily-like flowers 5cm across, faintly peppered with red. Lovely with *Adiantum aleuticum* 'Imbricatum', the prettiest low-growing, lacy fern.' This is typical Beth, clear-eyed, perceptive, wonderfully descriptive, never over the top but just right, and always putting the plant into context.

The late Christopher Lloyd, himself one of our greatest garden writers, hugely admired Beth's writing. He would often remark on her ability to capture the character of a plant, saying 'This is exactly the way it is.' Christopher and Beth were dear friends. They often visited each other's gardens, swapped plants, travelled together, exchanged regular letters and respected each other's work. Their gardening styles were quite different. Christopher lavished the medieval manor, buttressed yew hedges and tumbling outbuildings of Great Dixter with a no-holds-barred style that made you almost dizzy with colour. Beth's style is more refined, with elegant tapestries of contrasting shapes and forms and intertwined triangles reaching to the skies, creating an atmosphere of peace and tranquillity. Christopher recognized Beth's ability as a brilliant arranger of three-dimensional pictures. He was amazed at the ease with which she could analyse and paint images in her mind and on entering a garden could come up with streams of suggestions. Each inspired the other and a deep friendship blossomed.

Beth's years active in the Colchester Flower Club helped train and develop her eye. She recognizes a debt to flower arranging – particularly in the Japanese style – in her understanding of composition and form. This influence remains in her approach to design today.

Undoubtedly, a key influence was the late Sir Cedric Morris. The stylish and enigmatic self-taught artist entered Beth and Andrew's life in the 1950s. Morris had a keen interest in plants and lived and gardened, with his partner, Arthur Lett-Haines, in a rambling pink farmhouse on the outskirts of Hadleigh, in Suffolk, from which he ran the East Anglian School of Painting and Drawing. His collection of species plants was possibly the most extensive in Britain. But he also became interested in breeding new forms of the large border iris. He bred the first truly pink iris, seen on the Chelsea Flower Show stand of Messrs Wallace of Tunbridge Wells, when it was admired by the late Queen Mother, who allowed it to be named *Iris* 'Strathmore' after her childhood home. He also worked for many years on the wild scarlet poppy, *Papaver rhoeas*, aiming to create a blue poppy. Today this strain, in all shades from white through pinks to lilac, is familiar as *Papaver rhoeas* Mother of Pearl Group. He gardened freely, with artistic flair, but was also a careful observer of natural forms. His home, Benton End, became a magic place for the Chattos. Vibrant and intellectually stimulating, with an active and extended family of friends and students and a dreamy garden overflowing with interesting and unusual plants, Sir Cedric was also extremely generous. Many of his plants made their way back to Beth's garden.

Bringing plants home from the gardens of collectors such as Morris, and from her own travels, inspired Beth to propagate them. This drew her even closer to her material, and in time she set up a small nursery specializing in the unusual plants she had collected. At the time many of these plants were generally considered too weedy or wild to be ornamental, but there started the revolution. Through her flower arrangements, the garden itself, her writings and the magnificent Chelsea displays that stopped people in their tracks, Beth played a major role in changing people's taste in plants. She won ten consecutive Chelsea golds and, with the help of her brilliant propagator David Ward and a team of trusted and loyal staff, the nursery and garden grew not only in size but also in influence. Specializing in rare and unusual things, with hundreds of mouth-watering plants arranged according to their growing conditions, shape, colour and texture, the nursery is a paradise for plant lovers.

In 1989 Beth began the Woodland Garden, where shade from the mammoth oaks provides vital cover to rich assortments of woodland plants, and treasures from Turkey, Russia, Japan, China and North America rub shoulders with European natives. Here foliage is king and Beth's skill in creating exciting and intricate embroideries with contrasting leaf shapes, textures and colours is evident. Yet all is chosen with concern for the low average rainfall.

Soon after, in 1991, came the Gravel Garden. This for many was Beth's masterpiece, a collection of drought-tolerant plants beautifully arranged in emulation of a dried-up river bed, all on the site of an old car park. It began as a horticultural experiment on the sun-baked, sharply drained soil, to see which plants would survive and thrive without irrigation, in order to help visitors who might have hosepipe bans. It became the talking point of the British gardening world.

Now in her late eighties, Beth is still painting pictures with plants. Andrew died, aged ninety, in 1999, but his spirit and principles live on in Beth and in her garden. Beth continues to be active and is still the driving force behind her enterprise. The garden that has played such a large part in shaping British horticulture of the twentieth century remains as beautiful as ever and a place of pilgrimage for like-minded gardeners from all over the world. Beth's eyes sparkle, her wisdom continues to inspire, she continues to touch everyone she comes into contact with, lifting spirits, educating, comforting. Even in old age her life force burns bright. Greatness is not a word to use lightly, but in the presence of Beth Chatto we are in the company of greatness.

Fergus Garrett
Great Dixter
September 2011

Spring

As winter reluctantly retreats, the garden comes to life. The dormant season is over. Flowers emerge among the fresh greens, gently erupting from expectant buds and sharp-nosed shoots. The sun, often hidden behind a blanket of grey, or interrupted by fat cushions of white, occasionally shines bright, warming us with its glowing rays. Jackets and hats come off, only to be scrambled back on again as the weather breaks, cold alternating with warm, wet with dry. Whatever the weather brings there is joy in the air, as even the wooden, callused skeletons of the oldest trees come alive with thin veils of unfurling foliage.

Spring in Beth's gardens offers many moments of delight. Flowers fill darkened corners with hope. Crocuses pierce through the ground, opening wide with the faintest glimmer of warmth from rich orange anthers propositioning every bee. Carpets of wood anemones in white and blue cover the ground among the pillars of tree trunks; pink and plum-coloured Lenten roses hang their heads, hiding their speckled faces. Muscular daffodils shout for attention while the palest and most delicate of narcissus win our hearts. There are acid-green and yellow spurges, deep marine grape hyacinths. The musky orange bells of crown imperial fritillaries stand tall above their companions. Cherries flower delicately against a backdrop of green and the goblets of magnolia thrill every passer-by. Epimedium leaves marbled with coral veins hang from wire-thin stems, gargantuan gunneras erupt from prehistoric snouts furnished in layers of peachy-pink lace, and reptilian ferns hibernating in brown crowns unravel their fronds in slow motion. So abundant and varied are the textures and tones in Beth's palette that the garden is an invigorating mosaic of green. It is all very fragile: frost can in a moment blacken unsuspecting foliage, filling the air with the vapours of burnt milk as a Judas tree licks its wounds. But this unpredictability is part of spring's joy. The garden has broken its sleep, and soon this gentle awakening speeds to a canter of growth.

The filigree blossom of *Magnolia stellata*, a welcome sign of spring in the Woodland Garden.

The Woodland Garden comes into its own early in the year as flowers spring up to make the most of the sun before the leaf canopy forms. Here paths and seats are bordered by *Narcissus* 'February Gold'.

Hellebores create a rich carpet in the Woodland Garden: (left) *Ribes sanguineum* 'Albescens' overlooks the pale green *Helleborus argutifolius* (syn. *H.* x *corsicus*) and the coloured forms of *Helleborus* x *hybridus*, with *Narcissus* 'February Gold' in the background; (right) an opulent anemone-centred *Helleborus* x *hybridus* (picotee type).

OVERLEAF Delicate spring beauties (clockwise from top left): *Erythronium dens-canis*; *Narcissus* 'Jenny'; unfurling fronds of *Osmunda japonica*; *Helleborus* x *hybridus* (purple form); *Iris unguicularis* 'Alba'; *Ribes sanguineum* 'Albescens'; *Pulsatilla vulgaris* (shaggy petalled form); *Erythronium* 'Sundisc'; *Euphorbia rigida*; *Lysichiton* x *hortensis*.

Colour in the Woodland Garden: (left) bare branches allow woodland flowers to bask in the spring light; (right) the yellow-leaved currant *Ribes sanguineum* 'Brocklebankii' stands over hellebores and *Narcissus* 'February Gold'.

OVERLEAF Low spring sunshine gleams through the trunks of young oak trees, illuminating the blossom of *Amelanchier lamarckii*, *Spiraea japonica* 'Goldflame', *Helleborus* x *hybridus* and the pretty white bleeding heart *Lamprocapnos* (syn. *Dicentra*) *spectabilis* 'Alba'.

LEFT Striking foliage – the hosta-like leaves of *Veratrum album* and the golden, ribbon-like leaves of *Milium effusum* 'Aureum' – sets off the pale flowers of hybrid hellebores and the white currant *Ribes sanguineum* 'White Icicle'.

RIGHT *Pachyphragma macrophyllum* spreads a carpet of chalk-white flower clusters in the Woodland Garden as the snowdrops are fading.

OVERLEAF Exquisite spring flowers in the Woodland Garden (left to right): *Fritillaria meleagris; Lamprocapnos (syn. Dicentra) spectabilis; Leucojum aestivum* 'Gravetye Giant'.

LEFT Ash trees and the snowy blossom of *Amelanchier lamarckii* stand over the brighter tones of *Trillium chloropetalum* and *Lamprocapnos* (syn. *Dicentra*) *spectabilis* 'Gold Heart', threaded through with the blue haze of *Brunnera macrophylla*.

RIGHT Magnificent fritillaries, yellow *Fritillaria imperialis* 'Lutea' and the orange *F. imperialis* 'Rubra', growing among *Euphorbia characias* subsp. *wulfenii* in dappled shade.

PREVIOUS PAGES Paths in the Woodland Garden wind their way through rich growth of spring flowers and foliage including *Helleborus* x *hybridus*, pulmonarias, forget-me-nots and leaves of *Arum italicum* subsp. *italicum* 'Marmoratum'.

OVERLEAF White flowers light up the Water Garden in spring, with the blossom of *Prunus* 'Taihaku' and *Leucojum aestivum* 'Gravetye Giant' palely echoed in the ghostly bark of *Betula utilis* var. *jacquemontii*.

RIGHT *Prunus* 'Taihaku', thick with blossom, arches elegantly over *Leucojum aestivum* 'Gravetye Giant' and *Caltha palustris* var. *palustris*.

Against a backdrop of colourful spring flowers, light catches fresh new foliage in the Water Garden, with the shoots of *Gunnera tinctoria* emerging among the leaves of *Ligularia dentata* 'Desdemona' and *Bergenia* 'Rosi Klose' (below) and the slender fronds of the royal fern, *Osmunda regalis*, unfurling under the blossom of *Prunus* 'Taihaku' (right).

OVERLEAF In early April, fresh green foliage begins to veil the massive trunk of the dawn redwood *Metasequoia glyptostroboides* at the edge of a pool in the Water Garden, while in the foreground *Bergenia* 'Rosi Klose', *Narcissus* 'Thalia', *Skimmia japonica* 'Rubella', *Helleborus* x *hybridus* and *Symphytum ibericum* are in flower.

Summer

Summer brings with it a whole new feeling, calling on all our senses. The scent of roses, jasmines and philadelphus fills the air. The aromatic plants of the Gravel Garden exude their oils, bringing spicy aromas to our noses. Our ears are assailed by the sounds of euphorbias propelling ripe seed with loud cracks here and there as pods break open, casting their progeny far away. Magnificent *Stipa gigantea* makes a fountain of shimmering gold, while drumsticks of deep-blue agapanthus wave above the dusty gravel. Cranesbills, the hardy geraniums, spill out on to paths and sea hollies dazzle us with their metallic-blue colours. Impressive agaves are bedded out in strategic places to draw the eye. Silver astelias glisten in the sun. Helianthemums and cistuses open fresh flowers daily, as patchworks of colour come and go, while the seed heads of spent alliums, nectaroscordums and *Tulipa sprengeri* with its bleached capsules cracked open at the tips are remnants of a past scene. This is heaven, a dried-up river bed with an exotic maquis.

The delicate fresh greens of the spring have matured into deeper, sturdier tones. Now is the time for flowers. Pale pink phloxes, diaphanous veils of verbenas, arcane monkshoods, yellow after yellow of cheery anthemis, rich brick-red heleniums and powder-mauve campanulas follow one after another. As statuesque yuccas erupt into candelabras of white flowers, giant fennels zigzag to the skies on thick glaucous stems supporting balls of greeny yellow. The delicate cream froths of plume poppies dangle above fleshy grey-green leaves, verbascums light up like torches through the garden and clematis wrap themselves seductively around unsuspecting neighbours.

The long evenings are warm yet refreshing, offering respite from the heat of the day. The garden is filled with joyous colours as the countryside gradually turns brown. Beth's Water Garden provides an oasis amidst all of this. The damp hollow is deep verdant green, dragonflies hover over still water, and lush leaves creak as they move. *Thalia dealbata* with feet firm in the pond stands statuesque, casting impressive shadows on the water. Gunneras hold court, with mammoth leaves like Jurassic parasols; pink bottle brushes of bistorts brush against large phormiums. Trees are in full leaf; the woodland is dark with the canopy closed in. The spring cacophony of plants rejoicing in flowers has passed; the scene is calm, one of fine-textured ferns, gentle ground cover and subtle contrasts amidst the cool shade.

Beth's gardens change throughout the summer season as one complex layer takes over from another. The summer is long and brings with it anxious moments as areas of gravelly soil turn to dust. Plants are sheared and gracefully bounce back into life. Seeds are collected, vegetables are harvested, and plans are hatched for the coming season.

The sunny blooms of *Primula bulleyana* light up the Water Garden in summer.

BELOW In the light of a summer's evening in the Gravel Garden, the architectural silhouette of the stag's horn sumach, *Rhus typhina*, is surrounded by the delicate red blooms of *Tulipa sprengeri*, yellow *Phlomis* 'Edward Bowles' and downy mounds of santolina and *Ballota acetabulosa*.

BELOW Soft clumps of drought-tolerant plants are woven together in the Gravel Garden, with bright spots of colour from *Tulipa sprengeri*, pastel *Papaver rhoeas* Mother of Pearl Group, *Erysimum* 'Bowles's Mauve', the daisy heads of *Tanacetum niveum*, blue *Linum perenne* and the yellow-green of *Euphorbia characias* subsp. *wulfenii*, set against the muted grey of *Ballota acetabulosa*.

OVERLEAF Spectacular flower-heads and glorious colour in summer from (left to right): *Acanthus spinosus*; *Lavandula pedunculata* subsp.*pedunculata*; *Allium* 'Beau Regard'.

BELOW A path by a shady seat runs through plantings of *Verbena bonariensis* growing through *Libertia peregrinans,* its sharp sword-like leaves turning orange, and, on the other side, the blue haze of *Nepeta* 'Six Hills Giant' with *Stipa tenuissima* behind.

RIGHT In high summer the Gravel Garden is at its peak, with a riot of overflowing foliage and flowers. A triumph of natural gardening, it has never been watered since its creation in the winter of 1991–2.

OVERLEAF Soft, round shapes of drought-tolerant plants form a rich carpet in the Gravel Garden. Hovering above are the flowers on slender stems of *Lavandula angustifolia*, *Eryngium giganteum*, *Phlomis russeliana* and *Yucca* 'Nobilis', and over them a haze of yellow broom blossom from *Genista aetnensis* and *Spartium junceum.*

More architectural beauty on slender stems in the Gravel Garden, from *Agapanthus campanulatus* var. *albidus* (left) and *Stipa gigantea* (right) standing over the blue bells of *Campanula persicifolia* and mauve-and-yellow *Erysimum scoparium*.

OVERLEAF Pollinating
insects are attracted by
the blooms of (left to right):
Allium sphaerocephalon;
Gypsophila 'Rosenschleier';
Eryngium maritimum.

BELOW The Water Garden is an oasis of green on a summer's evening. *Prunus* 'Taihaku' arches over a grassy path bordered by the handsome foliage of *Hosta fortunei* var. *aureomarginata* in front of the shuttlecock fern *Matteuccia struthiopteris*, with *Phormium* flower spikes behind and the pretty blue flowers of *Pratia pedunculata* in front.

BELOW At the water's edge the dawn redwood, *Metasequoia glyptostroboides*, and *Crataegus coccinea* (the scarlet haw) shade the broad leaves of *Darmera peltata* and clumps of *Iris versicolor*.

OVERLEAF Lush planting in and around the natural ponds of the Water Garden includes *Pontederia cordata*, *Caltha palustris* var. *palustris*, *Iris pseudacorus* var. *bastardii* and *I. pseudacorus* 'Variegata'. In the background, late sun catches the lower branches of the golden larch, *Pseudolarix amabilis,* with the flowers of *Rosa glauca* and *Hebe vernicosa* on either side.

LEFT The planting surrounding this pool is enlivened by spires of white foxgloves and the golden tones of *Carex elata* 'Aurea' and, nestling at the water margin, *Mimulus luteus* and *Caltha palustris* var. *palustris* growing with *Butomus umbellatus* (the flowering rush) and *Thalia dealbata*.

RIGHT The moisture-loving *Trollius stenopetalus*.

OVERLEAF Summer flowers and foliage, mostly happy in damp conditions (clockwise from top left): *Astrantia* 'Buckland'; *Hosta* 'Halcyon'; *Euphorbia griffithii* 'Fireglow'; *Gunnera tinctoria*; *Primula japonica*; *Nigella damascena* (love-in-a-mist); *Dryopteris goldieana*; *Geum* 'Coppertone'; *Iris versicolor*; *Ranunculus acris* 'Sulphureus'.

PREVIOUS PAGES Under *Taxodium distichum*, the white spires of *Digitalis purpurea* f. *albiflora* add bright accents to the luscious rich green of the Water Garden. Stretching out into the water beyond the foxgloves is *Pontederia cordata* and, behind, a handsome stand of *Thalia dealbata*.

OVERLEAF Rich summer colour (left to right): *Papaver orientale* 'Cedric Morris'; *Primula bulleyana*; *Iris sibirica* 'Harpswell Haze'.

BELOW In early summer, the rose-pink *Syringa* x *josiflexa* 'Bellicent', mauve *Hesperis matronalis* (sweet rocket) and the white flowers and burgundy foliage of *Physocarpus opulifolius* 'Diabolo' make a harmonious colour grouping in the Water Garden.

RIGHT ABOVE The swamp cypress *Taxodium distichum* shades the pretty foliage of *Alchemilla mollis* that neatly edges the lawn.

RIGHT BELOW The variegated *Hosta* 'Spinners', pink *Persicaria bistorta* 'Superba' and *Iris sibirica* 'Royal Blue' create a pleasing contrast of form and harmony of colour in the Water Garden.

RIGHT AND OPPOSITE *Betula utilis* var. *jacquemontii*, with its striking shape and white bark, creates a focus in the green shade of the Water Garden. Colour comes from the rich red of *Primula japonica* 'Miller's Crimson', pink *Persicaria bistorta* 'Superba' and yellow *Trollius europaeus*.

OVERLEAF Drifts of moisture-loving flowers including *Primula japonica* 'Miller's Crimson', *Persicaria bistorta* 'Superba' and *Trollius europaeus* are threaded through the canal bed in the Water Garden.

Autumn

The luxurious days of summer are over; short days and long dark evenings are upon us. Warmth will soon give way to breaking weather, and killing frosts will switch the lights off. We prepare with greenhouses emptied and cuttings taken and wait with apprehension for the harsh realities of winter. Until then we can enjoy the misty mornings with fragile spiders' webs precariously dangling from vegetation catching beads of morning dew. Beth's garden takes on another patina with the joys of autumn. The soft furnishings of trees and shrubs orchestrate a mosaic of yellows, oranges, russets and fiery reds among evergreens well placed for contrast. The autumn tones are a feast for the eyes, with ornamental cherries glowing pink on orange, crab apple branches sweeping down to the ground heavily laden with fruit, roses randomly decorated with plump hips, liquidambers turning rich crimson red and *Ginkgo biloba* switching cloaks from green to butter yellow. Miscanthus sway in the wind with plumes of shimmering silver gold, the pencil-thin uprights of calamagrostis dominate the scene, and amber *Anemanthele lessoniana* spills into its neighbours.

Tender salvias glow against other plants. *Salvia guarantica* is rich velvety blue, *S. involucrata* 'Bethellii' soft textured and vibrant magenta, and *S. uliginosa* striking sky blue on upright elegant stems. The pink, mauve and white goblets of colchicums, naked without leaves, appear between shrubs and through low ground cover. Late summer perovskias continue to make an impression in a haze of smoky soft blue. The last of the monkshoods decorate the borders alongside late-flowering black-eyed and smouldering yellow rudbeckias and fiery persicarias. Mysterious toad lilies with curious speckled flowers lurk in the undergrowth. Scallops of anchoring bergenias spill out of the beds ready to turn liver-red and polished bronze as night-time temperatures drop. Seed heads and skeletons become our friends, not only feeding the birds precious seed, but adding structural decoration. *Phlomis tuberosa* 'Amazone', the spent heads of hydrangeas, teasels, sedums, arching crocosmias and little wonders like *Serratula seoanei* make us look again in amazement at nature's beauty.

Out In the vegetable garden fat cabbages sit plump-rowed with steely blue-green leeks set out like soldiers. Ornamental gourds are ready to pick. Seed harvesting continues, but the garden is getting ready for bed. Beth's garden will rest for a while.

The finely cut leaves of *Rhus x pulvinata* Autumn Lace Group begin to redden as autumn approaches.

LEFT AND BELOW The stunning autumn foliage of the elegant *Rhus typhina* makes it stand out like a jewel in the Gravel Garden. Striking, too, are the architectural shapes of the succulent *Agave americana* 'Mediopicta Alba' and the mountain gum, *Eucalyptus dalrympleana*.

OVERLEAF Autumn begins to transform this view of the Water Garden, seen in high summer on pages 64–5. Under the swamp cypress, *Taxodium distichum*, are pontederias and the dying leaves of hostas, while beyond is a tall stand of *Thalia dealbata* and opposite, backlit by the sun, *Gunnera tinctoria*.

In these two views of the Water Garden, autumn colours are beginning to appear, in the form of orange tints from *Astilbe chinensis* and glowing red from cornus (below), and the orange-red spikes of *Persicaria amplexicaulis* and the dusky seed heads of *Lythrum virgatum* (right).

OVERLEAF The large oval leaves of the tall and graceful *Thalia dealbata* and the sculptural foliage of *Gunnera tinctoria, Zantedeschia aethiopica* and *Pontederia cordata* are still green; but the leaves of the overhanging *Metasequoia glyptostroboides* and *Pseudolarix amabilis* are beginning to lighten, and the yellowing foliage of grasses and the seed heads of *Eupatorium maculatum* Atropurpureum Group, *Persicaria amplexicaulis* and *Lythrum virgatum* bring to the lush Water Garden a quieter, slightly wistful air.

The beautiful bark and dynamic trunk shapes of dawn redwood, *Metasequoia glyptostroboides* (left), *Prunus* 'Taihaku' (right above) and swamp cypress *Taxodium distichum* (right below) become more evident as autumn approaches.

OVERLEAF Glowing autumn foliage (left to right): *Cercis canadensis* 'Forest Pansy'; *Osmunda regalis*; *Taxodium distichum*.

RIGHT The white bark and fading leaf colour of the Himalayan birch, *Betula utilis* var. *jacquemontii*, gives it a ghostly presence in the Water Garden beside the softly reddening foliage of *Taxodium distichum*.

RIGHT The massive leaves of *Gunnera tinctoria* and the spiky foliage of *Iris laevigata* 'Variegata' frame an elegant boat floating above the reflection of an oak tree. The boat's colour is a pale echo of the blue of *Aster* x *frikartii* 'Mönch' on the bank.

Late autumn colour in the Water Garden (above) from *Taxodium distichum* and *Metasequoia glyptostroboides* and, in the foreground, *Persicaria amplexicaulis*; an oak tree, its leaves now a rich golden brown, is reflected in the still water (right).

BELOW The pale fading fronds of the shuttlecock fern, *Matteuccia struthiopteris*, light up the dark trunk of the swamp cypress, *Taxodium distichum*, with gleams of white *Leucanthemella serotina* behind.

RIGHT A mass of turning autumn foliage including that of *Darmera peltata*, hostas and *Carex pendula* surrounds the bridge over the canal bed.

OVERLEAF Autumn vignettes (clockwise from top left): *Pennisetum orientale*; *Stipa barbata*; *Crataegus coccinea*; *Ligularia* seed head; *Tricyrtis* (toad lily) flower; a robin on a eupatorium seed head; *Berberis thunbergii*; *Ceratostigma willmottianum*; *Pennisetum alopecuroides* f. *viridescens*; *Lythrum virgatum* seed heads.

The starry yellow flowers of the autumn-blooming *Helianthella quinquenervis* (shown left in close-up) and teasels, *Dipsacus fullonum*, stand behind the frothy ornamental grass *Poa labillardierei,* with *Amelanchier lamarckii* and *Miscanthus sinensis* 'Strictus' in the background.

The pale bark (left) of *Betula utilis* var. *jacquemontii*, and (below) the orange leaf colour of trees such as *Malus* x *zumi* 'Golden Hornet', the pale grassy yellows of *Calamagrostis* x *acutiflora* 'Karl Foerster' and the seed heads of *Phlomis russeliana* add interest to the Reservoir Garden in autumn.

RIGHT Under the straight trunks of *Amelanchier lamarckii*, *Colchicum* 'The Giant' brings autumn flower colour to the Woodland Garden.

OPPOSITE Low autumn sunshine shining through the branches of *Acer griseum* gives the woodland a romantic, almost magical air.

OVERLEAF Sun illuminates the elegant silhouette of *Cornus mas* 'Variegata' standing over ground cover of *Geranium endressii* and the fallen leaves which soften the paths in the Woodland Garden.

Winter

For many, winter is when gardens and gardening are at their lowest ebb. Bleak winds chill the bones, horizontal rainstorms lash the ground, soaking everything in their path, sodden vegetation sits switched off waiting for temperatures to rise, frost-bitten fingers function in slow motion. Life is hard, for the garden and for those who live and work in it. Battening down the hatches seems the only alternative. The greenhouse becomes a welcome retreat, providing a chance for frozen parts to thaw out while we visit old friends snug in their pots. Dark mornings and short days can make life dreary. Occasional fairy hoar frosts dust the world in powder, transporting us to another world. Snow comes and goes; sometimes, thick blankets bury the whole landscape, turning it a magical white. Food is scarce and the birds squabble over berries. It is time for precious repose, when thoughts are gathered, ideas formulated and spirits raised for the oncoming year.

But winter can be exhilarating too. The skies are blue and the air crisp, sunny mornings make you come alive, life feels good. The garden, although stripped to its bare bones, is full of interest and activity. Foliage, textures and shapes in different colours form essential soft furnishings. Marbled rosettes of silybum and galactites sit tight, close to the ground, lighting up dark corners. Intricately veined cyclamens glisten, awash with complex patterns of silver over green. The blue-grey-greens of rosemary, lavender, cistus and phlomis make comforting mounds on which the eye rests. The white-felted cushions of ballotas and filigree-leaved hummocks of artemisias become focal points. The dark, matte greens of conifers punctuate the borders, the black umbrellas of *Pinus radiata* silhouette the sky, with bamboos making fresh green fountains that sway with each gust of wind. A patchwork quilt of peeling barks from giant eucalyptus, layers of arching green leaves on stiffly bowing stems of self-sown spurges resting on their elbows, yuccas piercing the air, and colourfully striped New Zealand flaxes are all a part of this rich scene. Dogwoods and willows light up the garden with flaming red and orange stems glistening in the winter sun. And biscuit-brown grasses in russets and sparkling gold gently wave in the breeze, bringing movement and life. Liver-coloured bergenias spill out on to the paths. Winter irises, snowdrops, early-flowering Lenten roses and delicate jonquils burst out in pockets here and there. Hypnotic and heady scents from translucent yellow wintersweets, shrubby winter-flowering honeysuckles and prickly mahonias fill the cold air with hope.

Beth's garden in winter is rich with interest. Her ability to design using contrasting leaves, textures and shapes makes it as good now as it is at any other time. The effectiveness of the bare bones is testament to her ability and an example to every garden designer.

Snow coats the bright red stems of *Cornus alba* 'Sibirica'.

Snow outlines the sculptural forms of the stag's head sumach, *Rhus typhina*, in front of an ancient oak tree (right) and picks out its fruit-laden branches as they curve over *Phlomis* 'Edward Bowles' (left).

OVERLEAF The gate from the drive into the Gravel Garden opens on to paths and planting blurred and merged by snow.

The Water Garden is given a cold beauty in winter, almost all traces of the luscious, rich greenery obliterated, though enough remains – outlines of trees and shrubs and overwintering foliage – to give it interest through the shortest days.

OVERLEAF A frosting of snow and pale wintry sunlight give this view of the Water Garden an icy, eerie loveliness, making the scene look very different from when it was pictured in summer (pages 64–5) and in autumn (pages 82–3). The essential structure remains, with the stand of *Thalia dealbata* now a focal point in the expanse of water and framed by skeletal trees including *Taxodium distichum*. The *Thalia dealbata* will die down beneath the water after freezing, but will return in the spring.

PREVIOUS PAGES Winter jewels (left to right): *Callicarpa bodinieri* var. *giraldii* 'Profusion'; filigree snow patterns on *Taxodium distichum*; *Viburnum opulus*.

LEFT The appropriately named snow gum, *Eucalyptus pauciflora* subsp. *niphophila*, arches over a clipped holly, *Ilex crenata,* which stands in the wintry landscape like a natural Christmas tree.

RIGHT ABOVE Looking out over the water from the Reservoir Garden through curtains of weeping willow.

RIGHT BELOW The powdered green mound of *Mahonia* x *media* 'Lionel Fortescue' beneath *Betula pendula* in a snowy glade in the Woodland Garden.

OVERLEAF In the Water Garden snow blankets the paths and the bridge over the canal bed, accentuating the architecture of tree trunks and branches – such as those of the weeping willow *Salix babylonica* in the centre, *Taxodium distichum* to the left and the bamboo *Phyllostachys aureosulcata* 'Aureocaulis' arching over the bridge – and frosting the strappy phormium leaves and the low, grassy outlines of *Miscanthus sinensis*.

Books by Beth Chatto

Beth Chatto's Garden Notebook, J.M. Dent, London, 1988; Orion, London, 1998

Beth Chatto's Gravel Garden: Drought-resistant Planting Throughout the year, Frances Lincoln, London, 2000

The Damp Garden, J.M. Dent, London, 1982; Orion, London, 1998

Dear Friend and Gardener: Letters on Life and Gardening (with Christopher Lloyd), Frances Lincoln, London, 1998

The Dry Garden, Weidenfeld & Nicolson, London, 1978; Orion, London, 1998

The Green Tapestry: Perennial Plants for the Garden, Collins, London, 1989

Plant Portraits, J.M. Dent, London, 1988

The Shade Garden: Shade-loving Plants for Year-round Interest, Cassells Illustrated, London, 2008; previously *Beth Chatto's Woodland Garden*, Cassells Illustrated, London, 2005

Index

Acknowledgments

I would like to thank, above all, Beth herself, for allowing me the honour and privilege of access to her and to her gardens over the past years, and for all her help and encouragement in turning this book into reality. Thanks also to Tricia for being such a rock and for answering my countless calls and e-mails through tough and busy times; and to David, Aså, Chris and all the staff at the Beth Chatto Gardens, who were so endlessly helpful on every shoot.

I am extremely grateful to Fergus for his brilliant and perceptive introductory text; and also to Sarah Mitchell for her precise and elegant captions.

Thanks to the team at Frances Lincoln for having faith in my work and for making this book happen. I am very grateful to them all, especially to Becky Clarke, who immediately saw how my photographs of Beth's gardens could be brought together in a book, and to Anne Wilson, who designed the book so beautifully.

And a special word of thanks to the Central Line tube for bringing about an amazing chance encounter with Juliet Roberts, who introduced me to Beth. Without Juliet and *Gardens Illustrated* this book would never have existed. Big thank you to them – and professional hugs!

Finally and always, thanks to Joe for being Joe.

Rachel Warne
London
October 2011

The red form of *Anemone pavonina*.